BETTY CROCKER'S
CAKES
KIDS LOVE

GOLDEN PRESS / NEW YORK
Western Publishing Company, Inc.
Racine, Wisconsin

Choo-Choo Train

Cake: Heat oven to 350°. Grease and flour 6 small loaf pans, 4½x2¾x1¼ inches, and a round layer pan, 9x1½ inches. Prepare 1 package (18.5 ounces) any flavor layer cake mix as directed except—fill each loaf pan ½ full with batter and pour remaining batter into layer pan. Bake loaves 20 to 25 minutes and layer as directed. Cool. (Use round layer as desired.)

Frosting: Prepare 1 package (15.4 ounces) chocolate fudge frosting mix, Butter Cream Frosting (page 23) or Fluffy Frosting (page 23) as directed. On large tray or individual plates, place loaves top side down. Frost sides and tops of loaves.

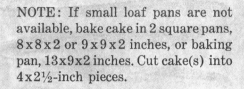

NOTE: If small loaf pans are not available, bake cake in 2 square pans, 8 x 8 x 2 or 9 x 9 x 2 inches, or baking pan, 13 x 9 x 2 inches. Cut cake(s) into 4 x 2½-inch pieces.

Trim: Use candy circle mints for wheels and a big marshmallow for the smokestack. "Fill" each of the 5 cars with one of the following: licorice rope strips, candy corn, miniature gumdrops, candy-coated licorice bits and chocolate pieces. To serve, cut each loaf in half.

3

PANDA

Cake: Grease and flour round layer pan, 8x1½ inches, and square pan, 9x9x2 inches. Prepare any flavor of our layer cake mixes as directed on package except —divide batter evenly between pans (batter in pans should be same level). Bake 8-inch layer 30 to 35 minutes and 9-inch square 20 to 25 minutes. Cool. Cut square cake as shown in diagram. On large tray, place 8-inch layer for body; arrange other pieces to form panda and place 2 large marshmallows on body for front paws.

Frosting: Reserve ½ cup frosting from 1 can of our vanilla ready-to-spread frosting. Frost head and body of bear with remaining frosting, joining pieces together. Blend 1 ounce melted unsweetened chocolate (cool) into the reserved frosting. (If frosting is too stiff, stir in few drops water.) Frost ears and paws and make circles for background of eyes with chocolate frosting.

Trim: For eyes, place slices of large marshmallow on chocolate circles; use chocolate pieces for pupils. Cut black shoestring licorice for claws; use black gumdrop for nose, red shoestring licorice for mouth and red gumdrop slice for tongue.

4

GIRAFFE

Cake: Bake our lemon cake mix in baking pan, 13x9x2 inches. Remove from pan and cool. Cut cake as shown in diagram. On aluminum foil-covered cardboard (about 28x12 inches), arrange cake pieces to form giraffe. (Use remaining strip as desired.)

Frosting: Prepare our creamy lemon frosting mix. Frost cake, joining pieces.

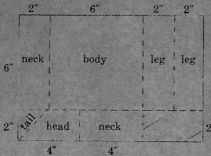

Trim: Sprinkle chocolate shot in "spots" of various sizes. Use black shoestring licorice for eyelashes, slices of small black gumdrops for hoofs, red shoestring licorice for mouth and peppermint stick candy for horns.

SAILBOAT

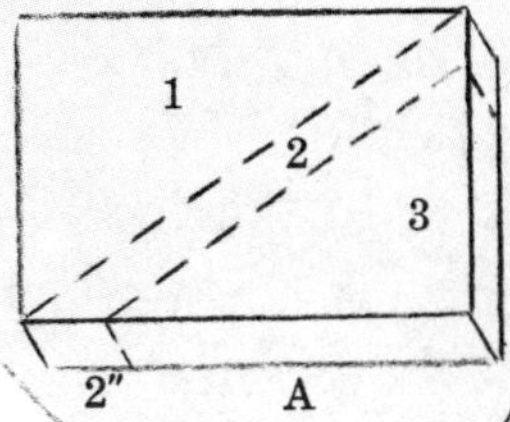

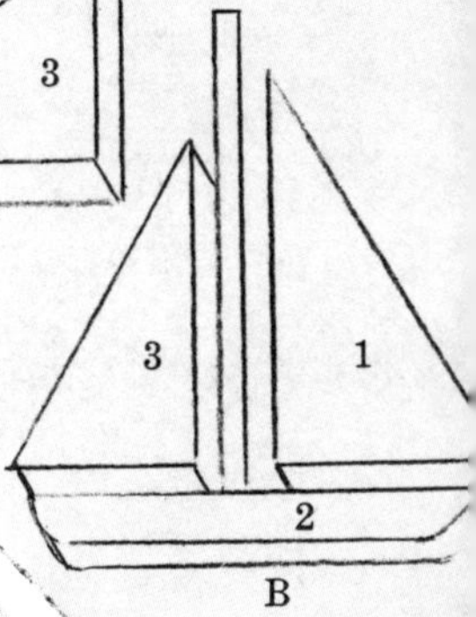

Cake: Bake
1 package
(18.5 ounces)
any flavor layer
cake mix in baking
pan, 13x9x2 inches.
Remove from pan; cool.
Cut as shown in diagram A.
On large tray, arrange cake
pieces as shown in diagram B.

Frosting: Prepare our fluffy white
frosting mix or Fluffy Frosting (page
23) as directed. Frost sides and top of cake.

Trim: Roll up 12x5-inch piece of colorful
wrapping paper for mast; secure and place between "sails." Use candy circle mints for rope
rings on sails and shoestring licorice for sail ropes.

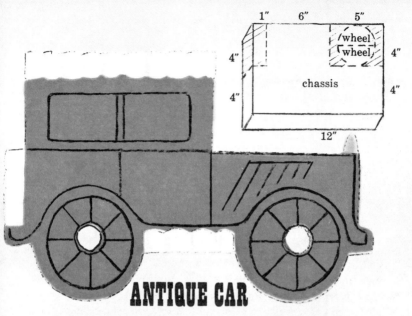

ANTIQUE CAR

Cake: Bake 1 package (18.5 ounces) any flavor layer cake mix in baking pan, 13x9x2 inches. Remove from pan and cool. Cut cake as shown in diagram. On large tray, arrange cake pieces to form car. (Use remaining pieces as desired.)

Frosting: Prepare any of our chocolate frosting mixes as directed on package. Frost sides and top of cake, joining pieces together.

Trim: Use shoestring licorice for windows, door, fenders and wheels. Outline running board, trunk and top of car with pastel-colored pillow candy mints. Use gumdrops for hubs of wheels.

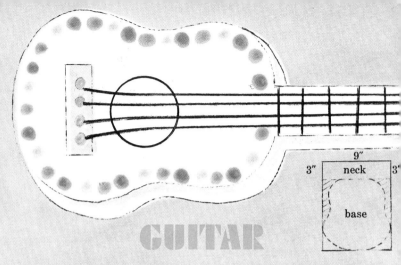

GUITAR

The diagram shows cutting guidelines: neck (9") and base dimensions (3" on each side).

Cake: Bake 1 package (18.5 ounces) any flavor layer cake mix in baking pan, 13x9x2 inches. Remove from pan and cool. Cut cake as shown in diagram. On large tray, arrange cake pieces to form guitar. (Use remaining pieces as desired.)

Frosting: Prepare our fluffy white frosting mix or Fluffy Frosting (page 23) as directed. Tint if desired. Frost cake, joining pieces together.

Trim: Use black shoestring licorice for sound hole. Sprinkle colored sugar in a rectangle, 3½x1 inch, below sound hole for string bar. Use short pieces of black shoestring licorice to make crosspieces on neck for fretted fingerboard. Place longer black shoestring licorice from string bar to top of neck for the strings. Place candy-coated chocolate candies around edge of guitar, on the string bar and at the top of the neck. Insert 2 small lollipops in each triangular piece at top for tuning pegs.

Chicken Little

Cake: Bake 1 package (18.5 ounces) any flavor layer cake mix in 2 round layer pans, 9x1½ inches. Cool.

Frosting: Prepare our fluffy white frosting mix or Fluffy Frosting (page 23) as directed. Fill layers with frosting. Cut cake in half. On large tray, arrange cake halves as shown. Frost cake with remaining frosting.

Trim: Decorate tail section of cake with lemon and orange candy slices. Break a yellow candy stick in half for legs. Cut circle of lemon slice for the eye. One lemon slice will make a wing, comb or beak.

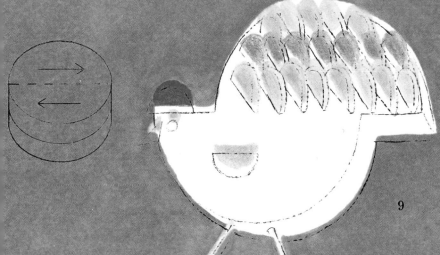

9

RAG DOLL

Cake: Heat oven to 350°. Grease and flour jelly roll pan, 15½x10½x1 inch. Prepare 1 package (18.5 ounces) any flavor layer cake mix as directed except—pour into pan and bake 20 to 25 minutes. Cool. Cut cake as shown in diagram. On large tray, arrange pieces to form doll.

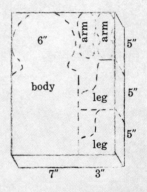

Frosting: Prepare our fluffy white frosting mix or Fluffy Frosting(page 23)as directed. Frost cake, joining pieces and rounding out head and sleeves.

Trim: Cut red shoestring licorice into ½-inch pieces for hair; sprinkle generously around head. Use slices of large black gumdrop for eyes and cut a triangle from large red gumdrop for nose. Make mouth, eyebrows and eyelashes with black shoestring licorice. Outline blouse and apron with black shoestring licorice. Sprinkle confection flower candies over sleeve, skirt and blouse area. Cut red shoestring licorice into 2½-inch pieces; place on legs for stripes on stockings. Sprinkle chocolate shot over feet for shoes.

To delight
a little girl,
don't forget
a candy
heart.

11

Gingerbread Boy Chase

Cake: Bake Gingerbread Boy Cookies (below). Bake any flavor of our layer cake mixes in 2 round layer pans, 8 or 9x1½ inches. Cool.

Frosting: Prepare our fluffy white frosting mix or Fluffy Frosting (page 23) as directed. Fill and frost cake. Decorate gingerbread boys as desired. At serving time, press hand of each cookie into cake.

Trim: Place gumdrop on top of cake above each cookie. For a birthday, insert candles in gumdrops.

Gingerbread Boy Cookies: Blend 1 package of our gingerbread mix and ⅓ cup lukewarm water. Chill dough 1 to 2 hours. Heat oven to 375°. Roll dough ⅛ inch thick on floured cloth-covered board. (Use small amount of dough at a time; keep remainder chilled.) Cut with floured 4-inch gingerbread boy cookie cutter. Place on ungreased baking sheet. Bake 8 to 10 minutes. Cool about 1 minute before removing from baking sheet.   *2½ dozen.*

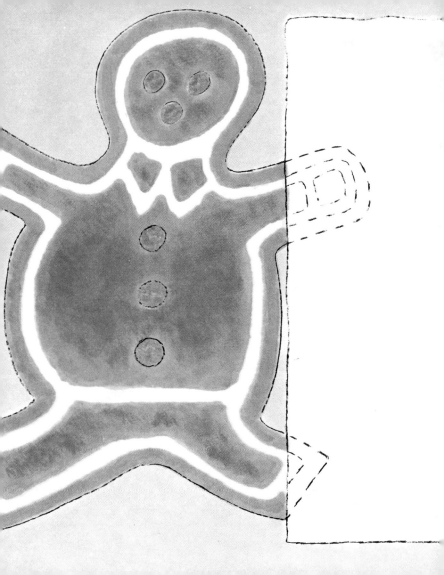

Cake: Bake any flavor of our layer cake mixes in baking pan, 13x9x2 inches, or 2 round layer pans, 9x1½ inches. Remove from pans and cool.

Frosting: Prepare our fluffy white frosting mix or Fluffy Frosting (page 23) as directed. Frost sides and top of cake, reserving small amount of frosting for making Cookie-and-Candy Animals.

Cookie-and-Candy Animals: On counter or large tray, arrange small cookies, candies, popcorn, peanuts, pretzels or marshmallows to form animals. Glue on faces with reserved frosting. (Cut gumdrops will stick without frosting.) When you have made an animal, pick up pieces and press onto side of cake. Decorate top of cake with gumdrops and candles.

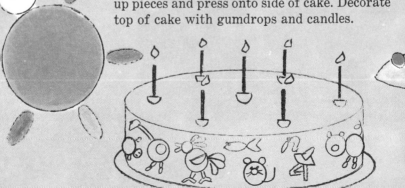

15

Cake: Heat oven to 325°. Grease and flour 1½-quart round glass baking dish. Prepare our golden pound cake mix as directed on package except—pour batter into baking dish. Bake about 60 minutes or until wooden pick inserted in center comes out clean. Cool 10 minutes; remove from baking dish and cool. Place cake top side down on serving plate.

Frosting: Prepare our creamy white frosting mix or Butter Cream Frosting (page 23) as directed. Tint frosting orange. Frost cake.

Trim: For eyes, use 2 slices of large marshmallow each topped with slice of large black gumdrop. Use another black gumdrop slice for nose; a large red gumdrop slice for mouth. Insert 1-inch pieces of black shoestring licorice for lashes around the eyes and ¼-inch pieces for whiskers on each side of face. Use curved black shoestring licorice for outlining nose area and eyebrows. Press chow mein noodles around edge of cake for mane.

LADYBUG

Cake: Heat oven to 325°. Grease and flour 1½-quart round glass baking dish. Prepare our golden pound cake mix as directed on package except—pour batter into baking dish. Bake about 60 minutes or until wooden pick inserted in center comes out clean. Cool 10 minutes; remove from baking dish and cool. Place cake top side down on serving plate.

Frosting: Prepare our fluffy white frosting mix or Fluffy Frosting (page 23) as directed. Frost cake.

Trim: Make face on side of cake, using chocolate wafers for eyes, slice of red gumdrop for nose, red shoestring licorice for mouth and black shoestring licorice for the eyebrows and the antennae. For colored shell of ladybug, sprinkle red sugar over cake about 2 inches from curved edge of "face." Place slices of black gumdrops for spots on "shell."

PARTY CUPCAKES

Cake: Bake 1 package (18.5 ounces) any flavor layer cake mix in paper baking cups. Cool.

Frosting: Prepare any flavor of our frosting mixes, Butter Cream Frosting (page 23) or Fluffy Frosting (page 23) as directed. Frost cupcakes and decorate in one of the following ways.

Butterflies: For each cupcake, cut a thin chocolate wafer cookie in half. Arrange as wings on cupcake by pressing curved edge of each half into frosting at 45° angle. Use silver dragées for eyes and pieces of black shoestring licorice for antennae.

May Baskets: For each cupcake, make a "flower" by cutting flat side of pink or yellow gumdrop into 5 sections, not cutting completely through. Carefully separate sections for petals of flower. Use a candy corn, tip up, for center. Place on frosted cupcake. For leaves, use green leaf gumdrops. For basket handle, shape a colored pipe cleaner and insert ends into each side of paper cup.

Menagerie Assortment: Slice and cut marshmallows and/or colored gumdrops into assorted shapes to form little animals, such as bunnies, bears, cats, fish, chickens, dogs. Arrange each on top of a frosted cupcake.

19

Toy Soldier and Clown Cupcakes

Cake: Bake 1 package (18.5 ounces) any flavor layer cake mix in paper baking cups. Cool.

Frosting: Prepare our creamy white frosting mix or Butter Cream Frosting (page 23) as directed. Frost tops of half the cupcakes. Remove paper cups from remaining cupcakes; frost side of each. Invert on frosted cupcakes and frost "tops."

Toy Soldiers: Invert flat-bottomed ice cream cone on cupcake for hat. Cut chocolate mint wafers in half; use half for visor of hat. Use black shoestring licorice for chin strap, red cinnamon candies for mouth, eyes and nose and candy wafers for ears.   *15 soldiers.*

Clowns: Use pointed ice cream cone on cupcake for hat, chow mein noodles or coconut for hair, sliced almonds for eyes and red cinnamon candies for nose and mouth. Insert small candy wafers for ears.   *15 clowns.*

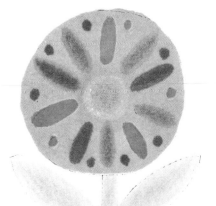

FLOWER POT

Cake: Heat oven to 350°. Prepare 1 package (18.5 ounces) any flavor layer cake mix as directed except—divide batter among 30 flat-bottomed ice cream cones, filling each scant ½ full (about ¼ cup batter in each). Place on baking sheet. Bake 20 to 25 minutes. Cool.

Frosting: Prepare 1 package (15.4 ounces) chocolate fudge frosting mix, Butter Cream Frosting (page 23) or Fluffy Frosting (page 23) as directed. Frost tops of cone cakes.

Trim: Insert lollipop in each cone cake; use green leaf gumdrops for leaves. Or, decorate cakes with candies, nonpareils or chopped nuts.   *30 cone cakes.*

Butter Cream Frosting

⅓ cup soft butter or margarine
3 cups confectioners' sugar
1½ teaspoons vanilla
About 2 tablespoons milk

Blend butter and sugar. Stir in vanilla and milk; beat until smooth and of spreading consistency.
Fills and frosts two 8- or 9-inch layers or frosts a 13x9-inch cake.

Fluffy Frosting

2 egg whites (¼ cup)
1½ cups sugar
¼ teaspoon cream of tartar or
1 tablespoon light corn syrup
⅓ cup water
1 teaspoon vanilla

Combine egg whites, sugar, cream of tartar and water in top of double boiler. Beat 1 minute on high speed with electric mixer. Place over boiling water (water should not touch bottom of pan); beat 7 minutes high speed. Remove pan from boiling water; add vanilla. Beat 2 minutes longer on high speed.
Fills and frosts two 8- or 9-inch layers or frosts a 13x9-inch cake.

DOLL HOUSE

Cake: Bake 1 package (18.5 ounces) yellow cake mix in baking pan, 13x9x2 inches. Remove from pan and cool. Cut cake as shown in diagram.

Frosting: Prepare our fluffy white frosting mix or Fluffy Frosting (page 23) as directed; tint yellow, pink or green. Use 9x5-inch piece for base of house, 9-inch side for front. Place triangles upright on base. Trim corners and base so pieces fit smoothly. (The pointed roof of the house will be slightly off center.) Use frosting to hold house together; frost entire house.

Trim: Use ½ cup toasted coconut or tiny colored candies for roof. Place row of chocolate chips (point in) where roof joins base of house. Use pieces of milk chocolate candy bar for doors, windows and panes. Use small candies and green leaf gumdrops for flowers and shrubbery. To serve cake, cut slices from roof section first.